THE ART OF
DRAWING HEADS AND HANDS

A GRUMBACHER LIBRARY BOOK

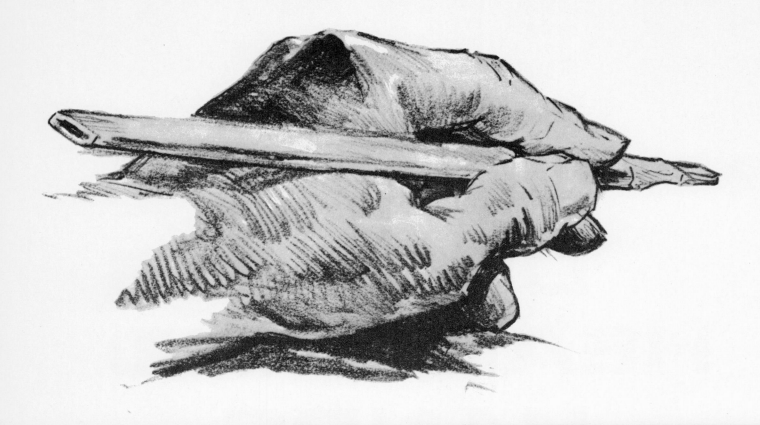

To supplement the text and provide quicker reference we include here a brief glossary.

ACCENT: Emphasis in a part of the design or composition, a sharp detail.

CAST SHADOW: The dark area that results when an object or form interrupts a source of light.

COMPOSITION: The arrangement of the various elements in a drawing or painting.

DRY BRUSH: A technique in which paint or ink is applied sparingly with a semi-dry brush.

FIXATIVE: A colorless fluid sprayed on pencil or charcoal drawings to minimize smudging. It can be applied by mouth atomizer or from pressurized cans. (Tuffilm or Myston)

FORM: The structure or design of an object or work of art.

GRAPHITE: A soft, black lustrous type of carbon. Used in lead pencils.

PLANE: A flat or level surface.

SPLIT HAIR TECHNIQUE: Pressure applied near the ferrule of the brush causing the hairs at the tip of the brush to spread out. This can also be achieved by rubbing the brush across paper until the hairs are spread.

STUDY: A detailed drawing or painting of an element to be incorporated into a finished work.

STUMP: Soft paper roll shaped at both ends and used for blending pencil or charcoal on a drawing. The Tortillon is spiral wound and shaped at one end only.

THUMBNAIL: A small, rough sketch used to plan composition before starting the finished drawing.

TOOTH: The surface texture of paper or canvas.

VALUE: Relative lightness and darkness.

VIGNETTE: A drawing or painting which is shaded to a soft edge.

WASH: A highly fluid application of color, lamp black, or ink.

Designed and edited by Walter Brooks
Copyright ©1966 by M. Grumbacher, Inc.
460 West 34 Street, New York, N.Y.
Library of Congress Catalog Card Number: 66-19000
Produced by Artists and Writers Press, Inc.
Printed in U.S.A. by Western Printing and Lithographing Co.

INTRODUCTION

Your interest and enthusiasm, and the urge to express yourself are the most important assets you can have when studying drawing. It is our hope that through this book we can help you to sustain your interest by giving thoughtful, professional direction to your efforts.

In drawing heads and hands it is more important to interpret character and gesture rather than to adhere slavishly to the realism of the camera. Your goal should be to make interesting drawings—so don't let the desire for highly rendered pretty pictures overshadow the more important spirit of animation, character, and vitality in your work. Your quick impressions, vigorous scribbles, can often capture these qualities and serve you better than tedious labored drawings. Detail is important only when it is related to these qualities—never as a substitute for them.

The artists who have prepared the drawings for this book, Lorence Bjorklund and Victor Kalin are excellent draftsmen whose years of experience with the subject lend great integrity to their work.

With a modest investment for materials this book can help you to better understand the structure, form and principles involved in drawing heads and hands so that your talent, coupled with effort, may bear fruit.

MATERIALS

The materials shown represent by and large what has been used in the preparation of the drawings for this book. You should begin with pencils. The degrees of softness or hardness of the lead will provide different kinds of texture on the paper, as will, of course, the paper itself. Drawing pencils are marked with either H (hard) or B (soft). The hardest is about a 9H and the softest a 6B.

In addition to round-lead pencils, there are flat lead sketching pencils and drawing materials that handle with similar ease, such as charcoal, carbon and artists' crayons. These, too, come in various degrees. Charcoal and carbon, available in both stick and pencil form, are excellent for rich blacks and varying textures.

To protect your drawing, use a fixative spray to keep it from being smeared. Fixatives can be bought in bottles for application by mouth atomizer or in the much handier pressurized can.

Kneaded erasers can be shaped in various ways for picking out details and permit you to erase without leaving erasure crumbs that have to be brushed from your drawing.

When drawing with pen and ink, it is usually better to start with a firm nib. The more flexible nibs require delicate handling to control the line, as they permit considerable variation in the individual stroke. Experiment with a few different points and also try using a brush to obtain a variety of ink lines and textures.

The stump or tortillon is used in conjunction with charcoal or drawing pencils. After drawing, the stump is used to rub the lead or charcoal into the grain of the paper, providing very soft blending of values.

Two of the most satisfying drawing mediums are Lamp Black Water Color and Sumi Black Paste Ink (Rend Ink). They are useful for quick statements, sketching on the spot, or doing finished drawings from your studies. Diluted with water, they both provide a complete range of gray washes. When used with just enough water to be workable, they give a rich black for either a fluid line or dry brush techniques. A round pointed red sable or sabeline brush is recommended.

There are many varieties of papers available:
Bristol Board—Kid Finish for pencil and brush; Plate Finish for pen and brush. Charcoal Paper—white and colors. Water Color Papers—Cold Pressed (CP); Rough (R); Hot Pressed (HP). Illustration Board—Cold Pressed (CP) and Smooth.
These papers are available as sheets, pads and sketch books.

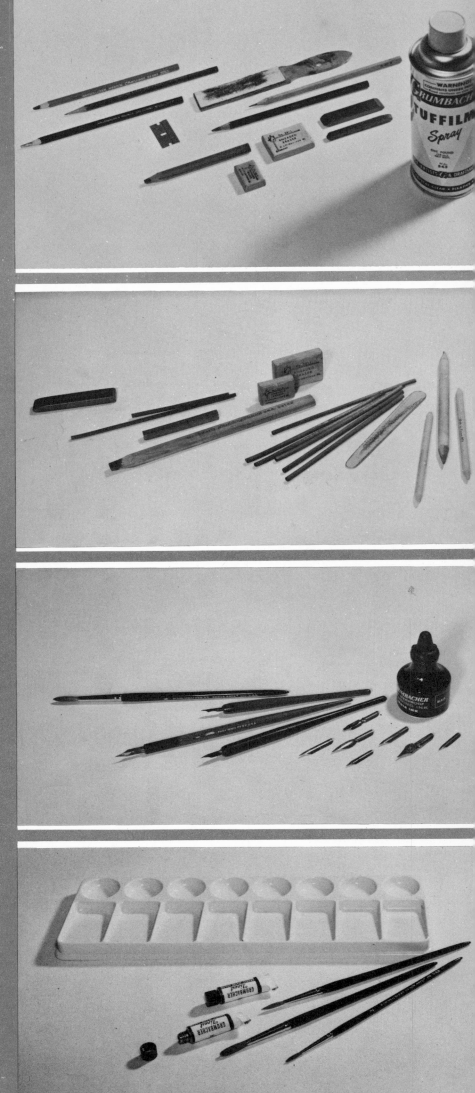

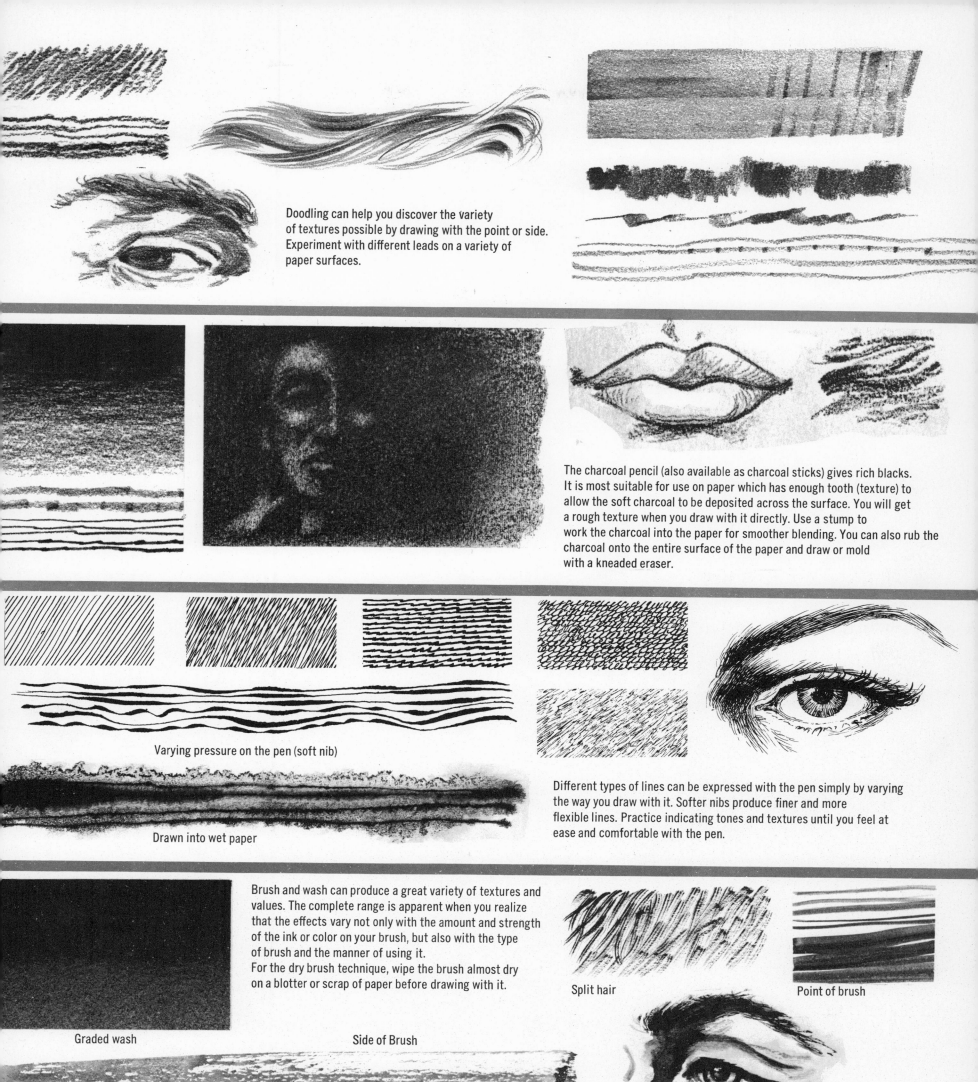

Doodling can help you discover the variety of textures possible by drawing with the point or side. Experiment with different leads on a variety of paper surfaces.

The charcoal pencil (also available as charcoal sticks) gives rich blacks. It is most suitable for use on paper which has enough tooth (texture) to allow the soft charcoal to be deposited across the surface. You will get a rough texture when you draw with it directly. Use a stump to work the charcoal into the paper for smoother blending. You can also rub the charcoal onto the entire surface of the paper and draw or mold with a kneaded eraser.

Varying pressure on the pen (soft nib)

Drawn into wet paper

Different types of lines can be expressed with the pen simply by varying the way you draw with it. Softer nibs produce finer and more flexible lines. Practice indicating tones and textures until you feel at ease and comfortable with the pen.

Brush and wash can produce a great variety of textures and values. The complete range is apparent when you realize that the effects vary not only with the amount and strength of the ink or color on your brush, but also with the type of brush and the manner of using it.
For the dry brush technique, wipe the brush almost dry on a blotter or scrap of paper before drawing with it.

Split hair

Point of brush

Graded wash

Side of Brush

[5]

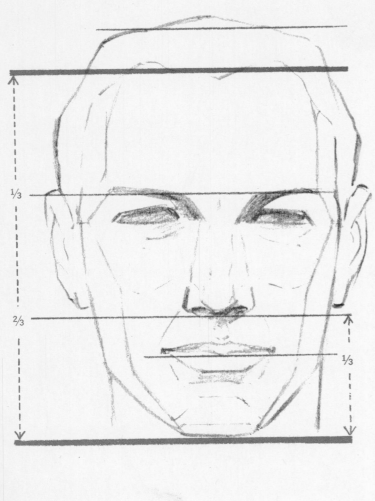

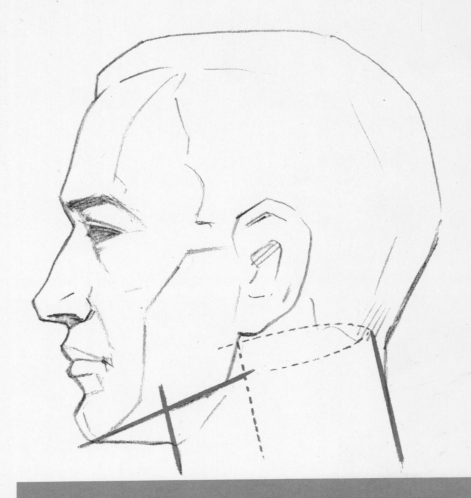

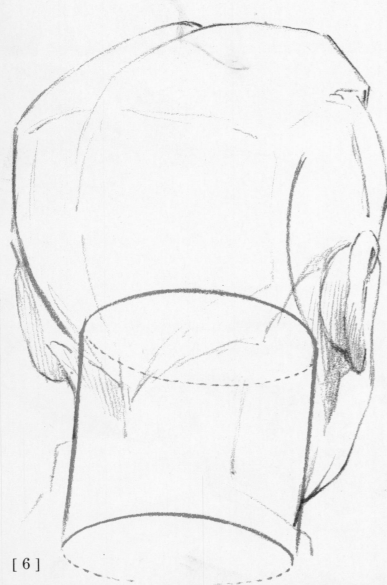

A basic knowledge of the skull, muscle structure and planes of the head is important in analyzing the subject you are drawing.

The ideal proportions shown here should be considered in the broadest sense. They are a guide to getting started. It is the variations in these proportions which establish the characteristics which make one person different from another.

Proportionally, the distance from the chin to the tip of the nose, nose to brow and brow to hairline should be equal. The width of the face at the eyes is equal to the distance from the eyebrows to the bottom of the chin. The mouth is one third the distance from the nose to the chin and ideally this distance is equal to that from the hairline to the top of the skull.

The head is flat on the sides, and the ears which join above the hinge of the jaw are equal in length to the distance from the tip of the nose to the line of the eyebrows.

A proper positioning of the head on the neck is very important. As can be seen in the profile drawing, the ball of the head sits on the tubular neck form at a point in line with the ear; the jaw protrudes from slightly off center of this at an angle to the chin. Notice also the joining of neck and head as viewed from the back.

The female head follows these same general proportions without the angular quality. Softness of form is characteristic of women and children.

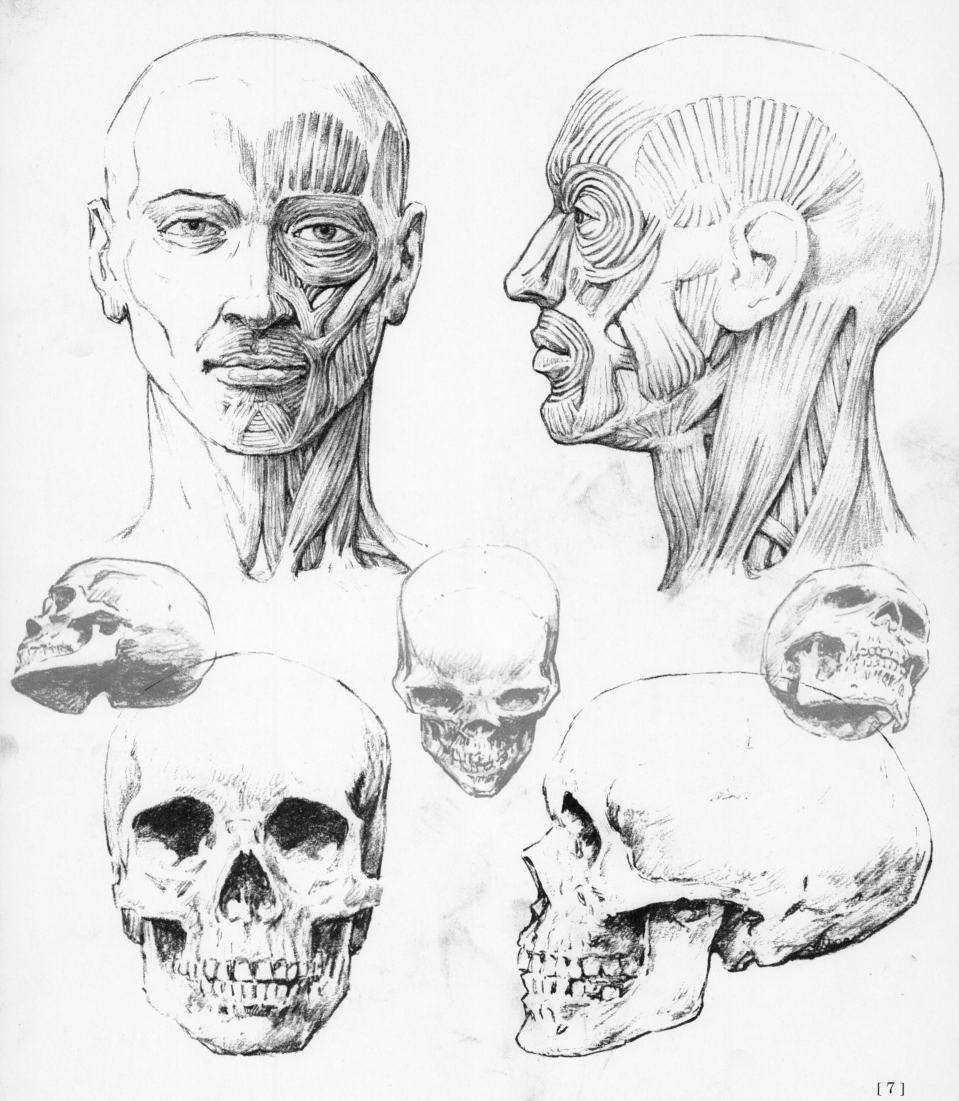

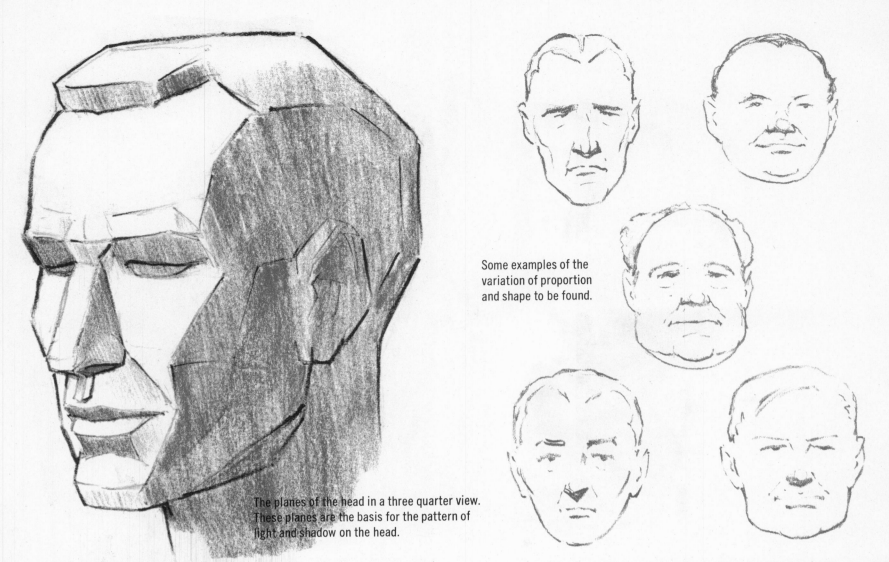

Some examples of the variation of proportion and shape to be found.

The planes of the head in a three quarter view. These planes are the basis for the pattern of light and shadow on the head.

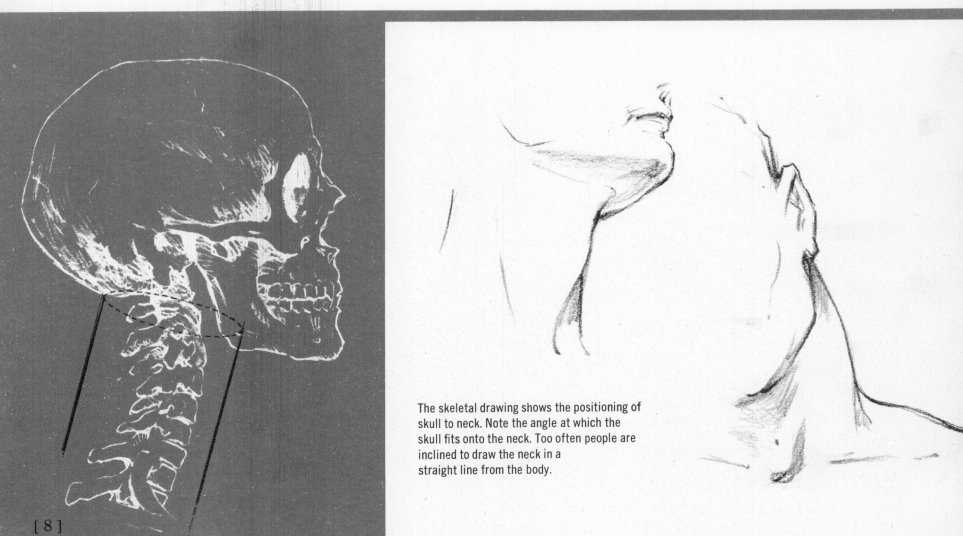

The skeletal drawing shows the positioning of skull to neck. Note the angle at which the skull fits onto the neck. Too often people are inclined to draw the neck in a straight line from the body.

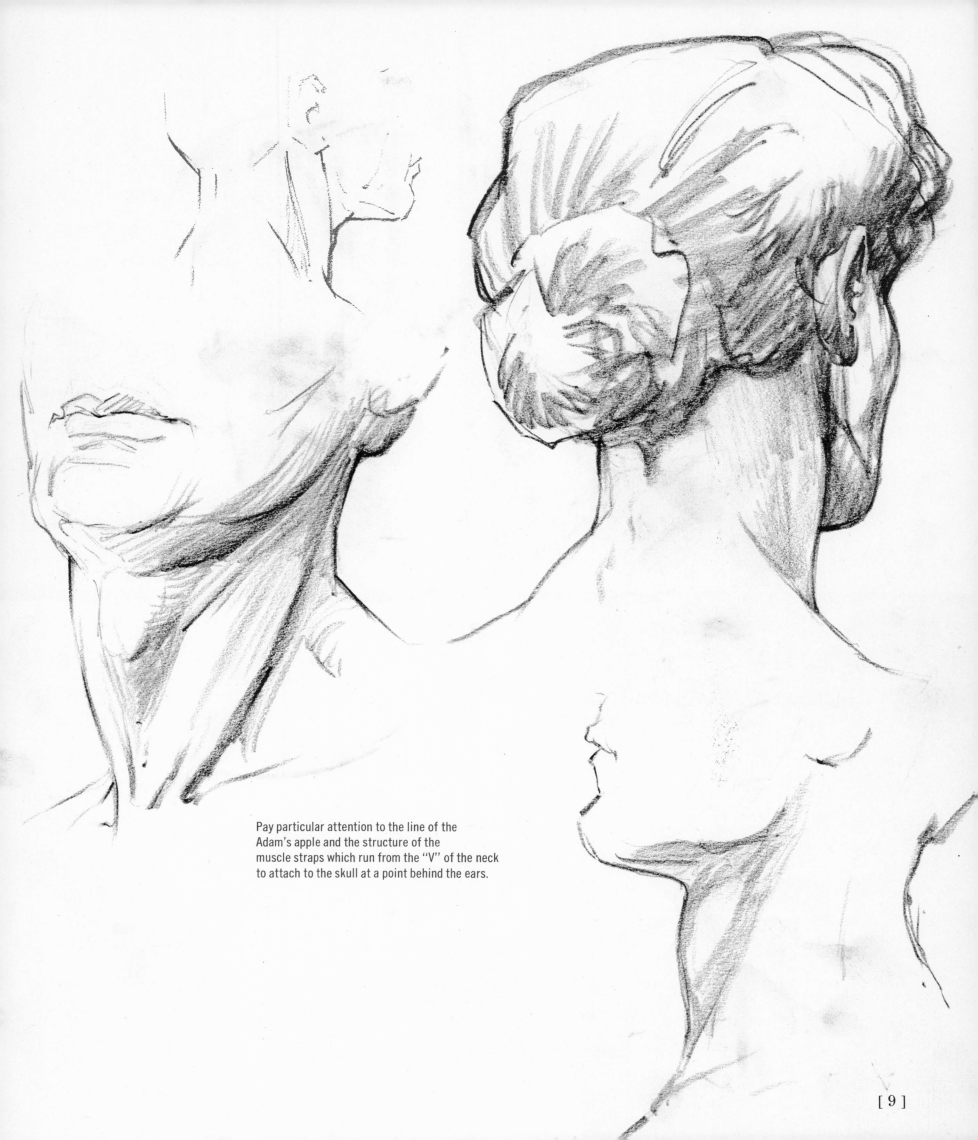

Pay particular attention to the line of the Adam's apple and the structure of the muscle straps which run from the "V" of the neck to attach to the skull at a point behind the ears.

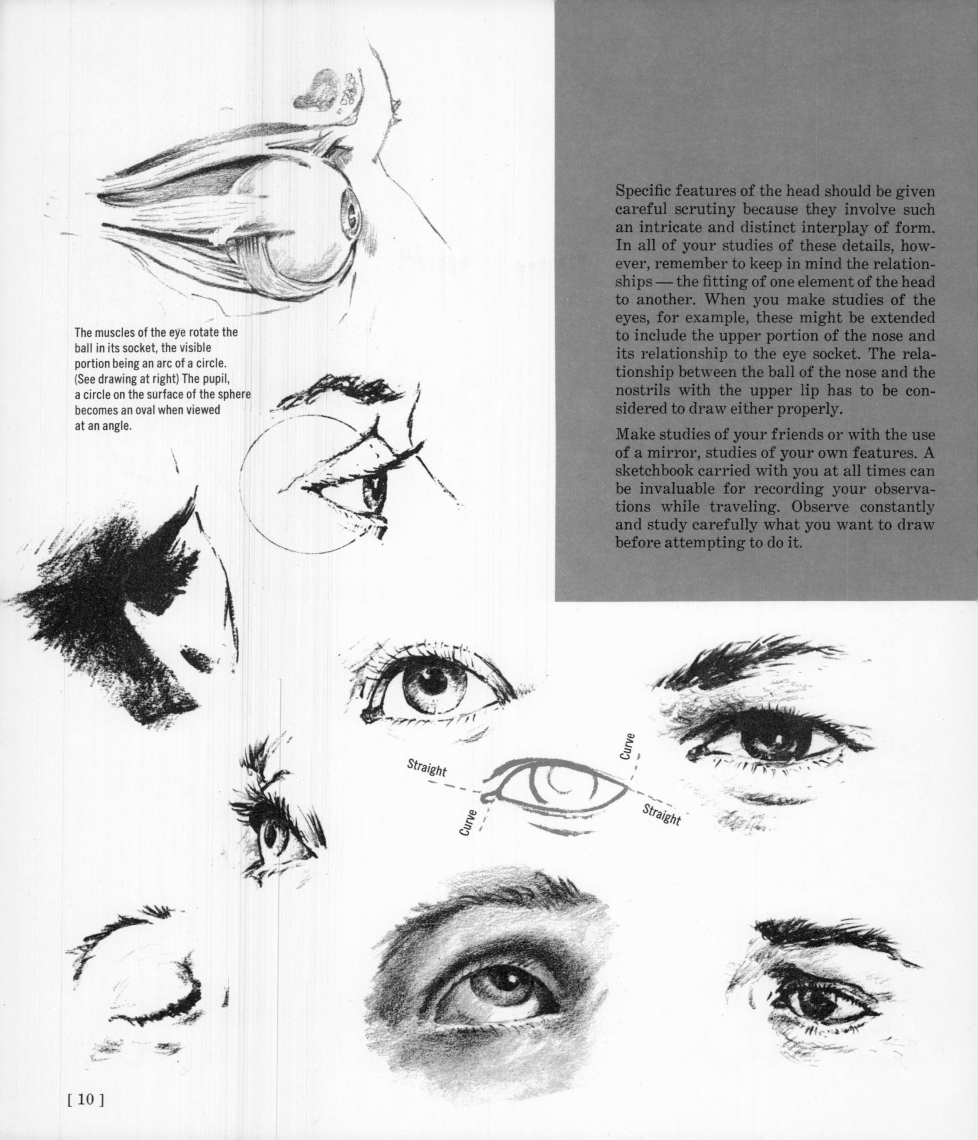

The muscles of the eye rotate the ball in its socket, the visible portion being an arc of a circle. (See drawing at right) The pupil, a circle on the surface of the sphere becomes an oval when viewed at an angle.

Specific features of the head should be given careful scrutiny because they involve such an intricate and distinct interplay of form. In all of your studies of these details, however, remember to keep in mind the relationships — the fitting of one element of the head to another. When you make studies of the eyes, for example, these might be extended to include the upper portion of the nose and its relationship to the eye socket. The relationship between the ball of the nose and the nostrils with the upper lip has to be considered to draw either properly.

Make studies of your friends or with the use of a mirror, studies of your own features. A sketchbook carried with you at all times can be invaluable for recording your observations while traveling. Observe constantly and study carefully what you want to draw before attempting to do it.

Straight

Curve

Curve

Straight

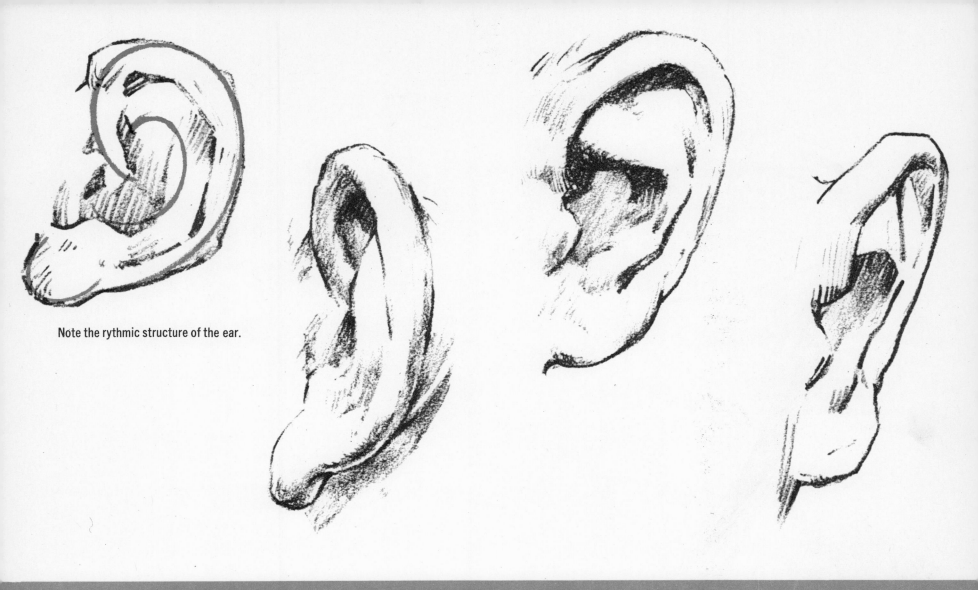

Note the rythmic structure of the ear.

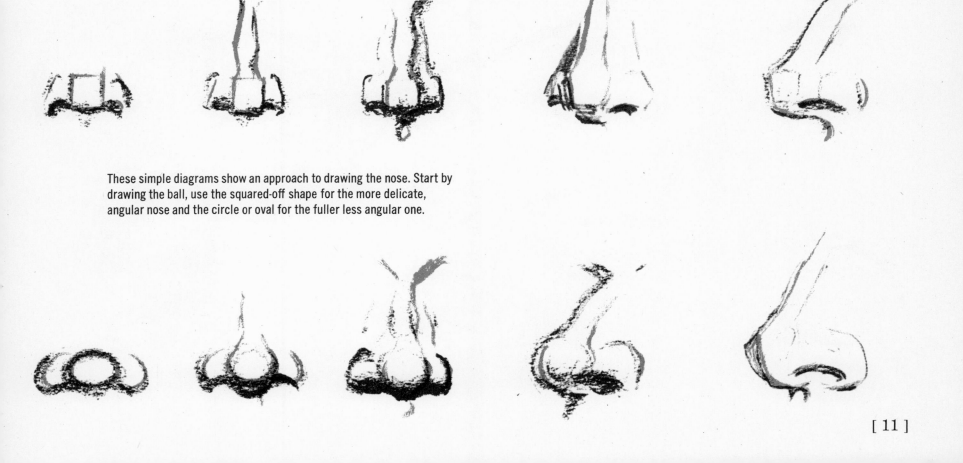

These simple diagrams show an approach to drawing the nose. Start by drawing the ball, use the squared-off shape for the more delicate, angular nose and the circle or oval for the fuller less angular one.

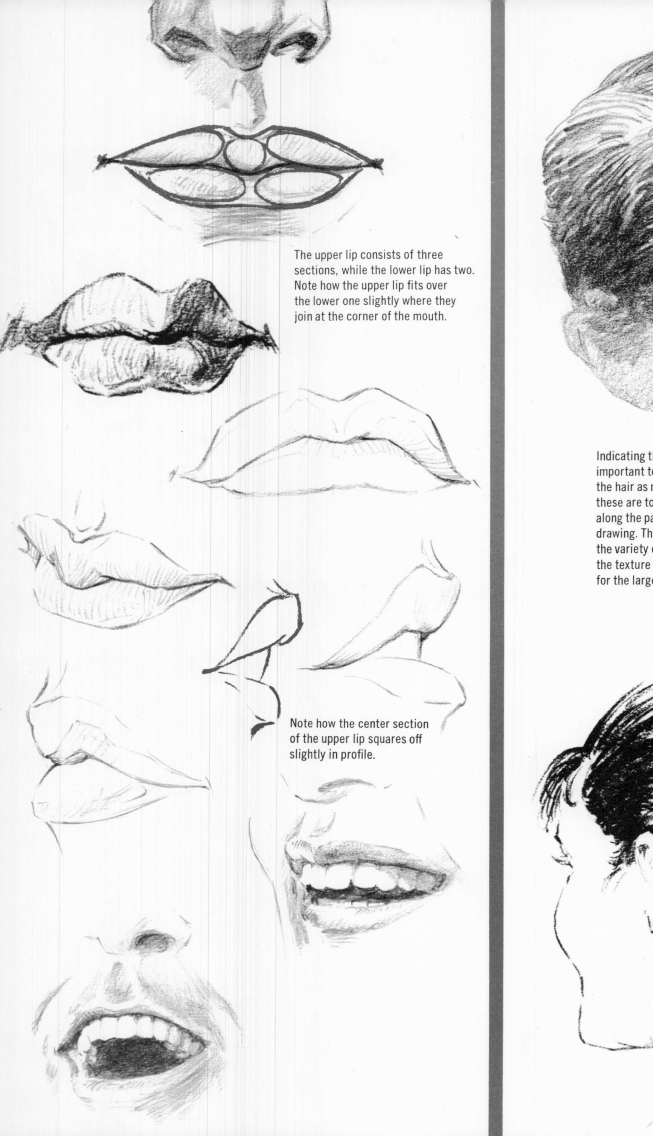

The upper lip consists of three sections, while the lower lip has two. Note how the upper lip fits over the lower one slightly where they join at the corner of the mouth.

Note how the center section of the upper lip squares off slightly in profile.

Indicating the form and texture of hair properly is as important to your drawing as any other feature. Draw the hair as masses from the point of origin. In most cases these are toward the back of the head, the hairline, or along the part — depending upon the view of the head you are drawing. This same principle holds true even with the variety of arrangements in women's hair. Indicate the texture and form in the darker areas; look for the larger clusters.

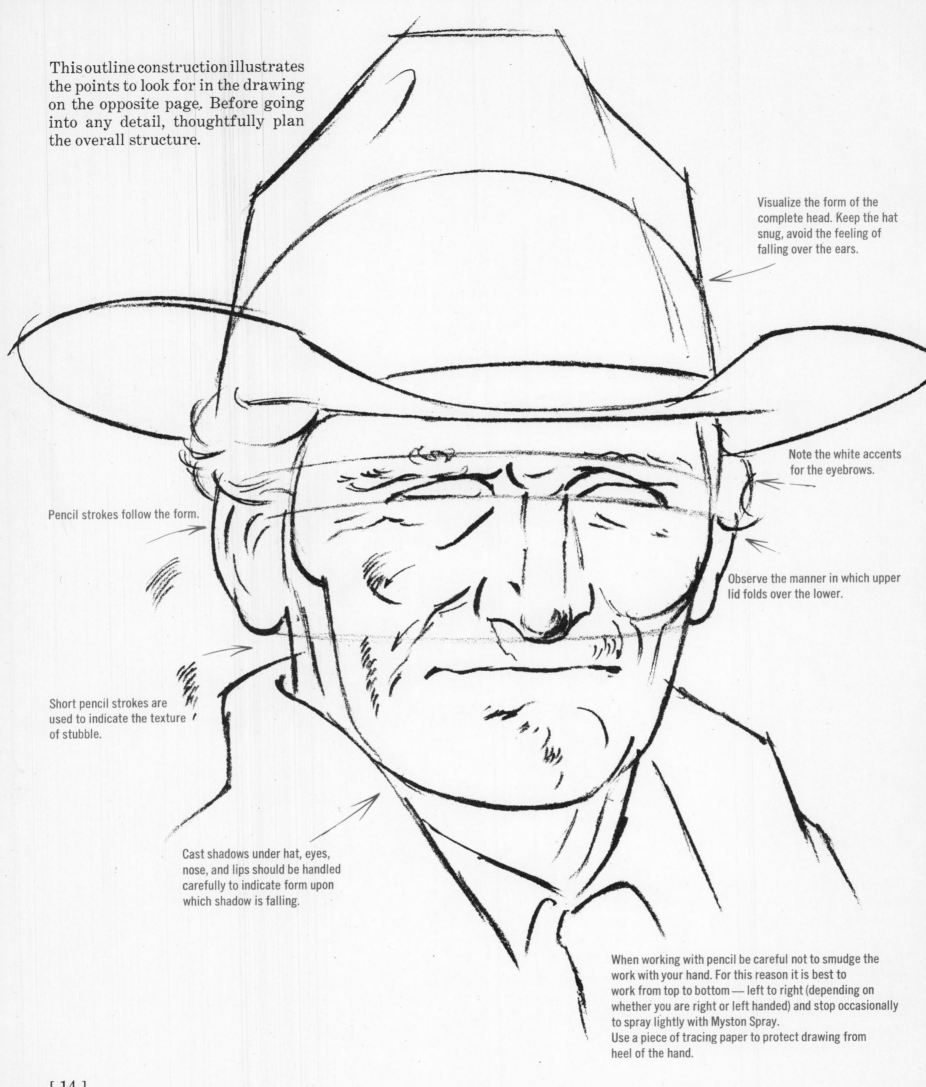

This outline construction illustrates the points to look for in the drawing on the opposite page. Before going into any detail, thoughtfully plan the overall structure.

Visualize the form of the complete head. Keep the hat snug, avoid the feeling of falling over the ears.

Note the white accents for the eyebrows.

Pencil strokes follow the form.

Observe the manner in which upper lid folds over the lower.

Short pencil strokes are used to indicate the texture of stubble.

Cast shadows under hat, eyes, nose, and lips should be handled carefully to indicate form upon which shadow is falling.

When working with pencil be careful not to smudge the work with your hand. For this reason it is best to work from top to bottom — left to right (depending on whether you are right or left handed) and stop occasionally to spray lightly with Myston Spray.
Use a piece of tracing paper to protect drawing from heel of the hand.

This study would be a good one to try because of the interesting problems in form, texture, cast shadow and structure that it presents. As you draw, watch carefully edges where forms connect or pass each other. Think constantly in terms of the shape you are drawing and feel the turns and structure as you work with your pencil. Try this on Kid Finish Bristol Board and rougher paper surfaces.

The head above was drawn with a split hair technique on a Plate Finish Bristol Board. A light penciling in of the structure (shown on the right) served as a foundation for rendering the form. As with pencil drawing note how strokes follow form throughout.

This technique is achieved by dipping the brush in ink and then pressing the heel (where the hair joins the ferrule) with your finger against a scrap of paper or blotter. In A the brush is very dry and texture is indicated with tip. In B the side of the brush was used with slightly more ink. In C the tip of the brush was used, hairs split as previously described.

A

B

C

The drawing above shows the charcoal pencil used without
employing a stump on a cold pressed Illustration Board.
The one on the left shows the effect of rubbing charcoal
into the grain of the paper. Note the simplicity with which
the character has been expressed — detail kept to a minimum.
The swatch below illustrates the results of rubbing with the
stump and the possibilities for re-stating dark areas
within this value.

2B pencil on Bond paper

Your studies need not always concentrate on the face. Try studies of the back of the head. Pay attention to the angle or tilt and the position of the shoulders.

The felt tip pen was used for the portrait shown. Quickly stated, it expresses the essence of the subject without drawing the entire head.

Felt tip pen on Bond paper

Looking at your subject through half closed eyes will eliminate unnecessary detail and help you to see and to state it in its simplest terms.

Felt tip pen on Bond paper

2B pencil on Bond paper

It isn't necessary to use a hard outline. If the structure
is right and emphasis placed in the shadow areas
(under lips, nose, etc.) the head will hold together.
This is an especially effective approach when doing drawings
on toned paper.

The drawing at the left is an example of using the
kneaded eraser to pick out details of the drawing after the
charcoal has been rubbed into the grain of the paper.
Black accents can be restated for additional dimension.

Charcoal pencil on charcoal paper

It isn't necessary to draw out the ball and structure each time. With experience a visualization of the edges and a general breakdown of the form can be enough structure to start building up detail.

In the drawing above, the strong light washes out detail on the left, while on the right, a softer reflected light brings out detail in the dark area.

Some of these heads might be tried for experience using different techniques such as the split hairbrush or working with the stump on a variety of papers.

Felt tip pen on Bond paper

In working with the felt tip pen state all of the darkest areas first and work outward. This will dry out the tip slightly so that the middle values and more delicate areas of your drawing can be indicated.

Felt tip pen on Plate Finish Bristol Board

2B pencil on Bond paper

2B pencil on charcoal paper

Charcoal pencil on
Michelangelo charcoal paper

Charcoal pencil on
Michelangelo
charcoal paper

Felt tip pen on Bond paper

Felt tip pen on Plate Finish Bristol Board
Black accents Dry Brush

[23]

A prime consideration when drawing younger women is the matter of what to leave out rather than what to put in. This has nothing to do with the lady's vanity. Your attempts to express the vitality and charm of the subject will miss if your drawing overemphasizes structure. This is especially true of the form of the upper lip and the line which runs from the edge of the nostril to the corner of the mouth. Details which should be emphasized are eyes, lips and hair. The structure of the head stated in the simplest terms possible without an overworking of the form will generally be more successful.

Pen and ink on Plate Finish Bristol Board

"Cartoonist" pencil on Charcoal Paper

Wash drawing on illustration board

Wash drawing on illustration board

In these drawings note how simply the form is expressed. The entire bulk and dimension of the head is carried by the proper placing of the features and the manner in which the hair is drawn. Emphasis is kept on eyes, lips and hair.

The above drawings in wash use the "Cartoonist" pencil for additional value and texture. The "Cartoonist" pencil was used for the drawing on the right.

In all of these drawings note how the form of the nose and face is kept very simple with emphasis on hair, eyes and lips and their proper placement.

A fine example of understating form can be seen in the very expressive pen and ink drawing above. The entire left side of the face is implied by the manner in which the features are placed.

With older women it is necessary to state more of the form.
However, there is a softness to this form. Hard accents
should be brought in only where you want to indicate the
edge of a plane, as at the line of the jaw.
A good touch for indicating the softness at the back of the
neck is by delicately defining the ends of the hair.

One characteristic of babies and young children is a roundness and softness of form. As with young women you will find that understating certain aspects and concentrating on others will express the subject much better. Proper placement of the eyes, ball of the nose and the mouth in the head goes a long way toward establishing the drawing. An emphasis on form in the cheek or upper lip has a tendency to take on a grotesque quality.

Because the jaw hasn't developed, proportion in the overall features is quite different from that in the adult face. The brow line is about half the distance from the top of the skull to the chin. If you divide this distance from brow line and chin into quarters, the lower rim of the eyes would be at the first quarter, the bottom of the nose at one half, and the bottom of the lower lip at a line three quarters of the distance.

The nose is small and the eyes large in proportion to the overall face. Ears, too, are smaller and located in relation to the line of the brow and tip of the nose slightly lower than in the adult. The neck is also smaller in relation to the head.

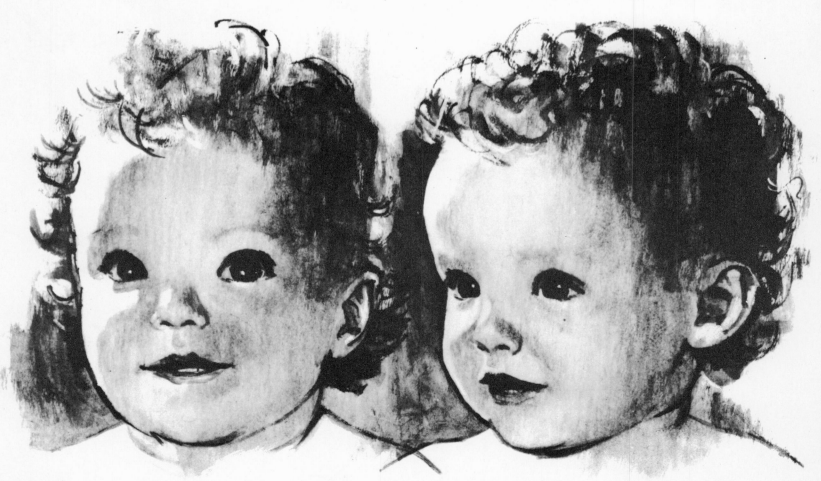

Rather than hope that your subject will stop moving, concentrate on observing at great length before you start to draw.

In this brush and ink drawing a delicate line is used in combination with a dry brush technique. The form of the head is understated relying on the drawing of the hair, eyes, nose and mouth to express the character.

The swatches below show how some of the effects in the drawing were achieved.

In A the side of a semi dry brush was used. In B the tip of a very fluid brush was used. This is the manner in which the hair was put in, drawing in the direction of the growth. The light accents were scratched in with a razor blade after the ink had dried. In C we see how a softer tone can be indicated with the razor blade. The gray value in the pupils was handled this way.

A

B

C

The pen and ink drawings on the left are excellent examples of how freely the subject can be expressed. Don't be afraid of making a bad drawing or putting down a line in the wrong place in your attempts to express the movement and character of the subject. The drawing on the right was executed on Canvas grain paper using brush techniques.

Sumi Chinese Paste Ink (Rend Ink) was used on a smooth textured illustration board for this drawing. Note the simplicity and restraint with which the form is stated.

As children grow, the jaw and neck develop and the proportions of the face become closer to that of the adult.

Sumi Ink was used on Capri Rough (R) Water Color Paper for this drawing. The delineation of form in this head shows how subtly this must be handled to be effective. Even with this amount of modeling the handling within the dark areas is kept very direct and simple.

It is more important to state the gesture or attitude than develop a highly finished drawing. Your observation and a few well stated lines can capture this vital quality to be carried over to more finished drawings.

[35]

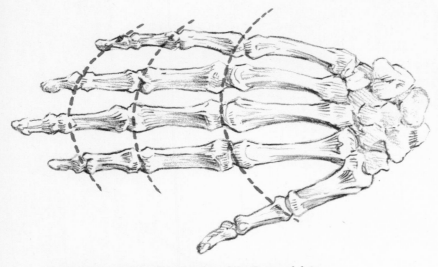

Notice the arcs formed by the tips of the fingers, joints and knuckles. Pay attention to the tapering of each segment and their size relationships.

The skeletal and muscular structure of the hand is presented here to familiarize you with how it affects what you see and therefore what you draw. Since our intention is to deal in visual experience rather than medical terms, we suggest that you start by making a tracing of your own hand spread out flat on a piece of paper. As you trace, observe where knuckles and joints fall. Now take your hand from the tracing and use it as a model for the corrections and adjustments needed to make what you traced look like a drawing. By the use of a mirror you have an excellent model for your studies of the hand that isn't busy drawing.

When drawing the hand, the time spent in careful observation, developing a feeling for the relationship and proportion of the various parts of the hand and making many quick studies, is much better than trying to do more finished drawings at the start.

In the second color below, the tendons of the hand are shown. With age these become more prominent as do the blood vessels in the back of the hand. This is especially true with men.

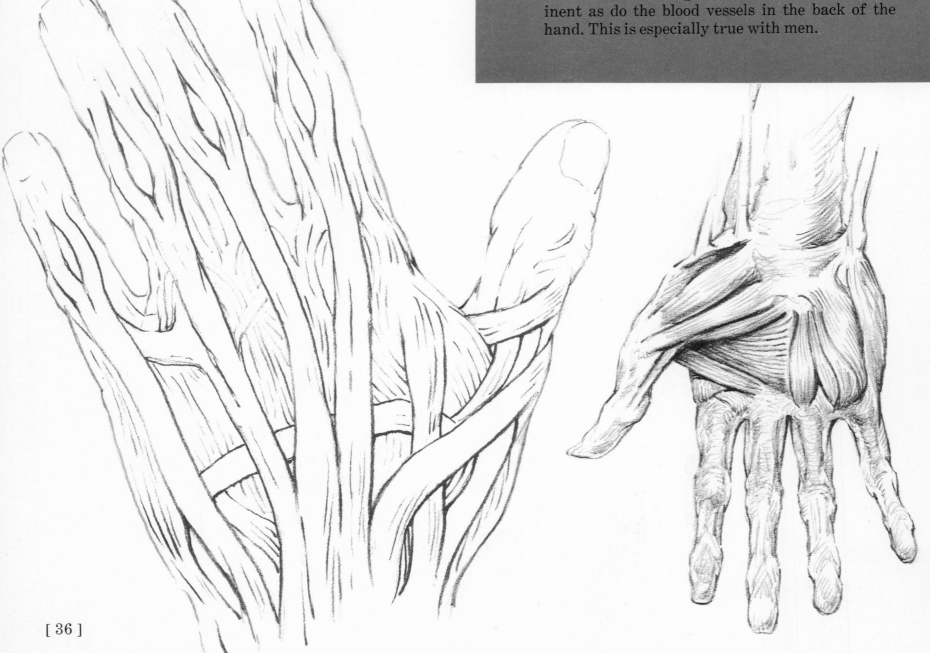

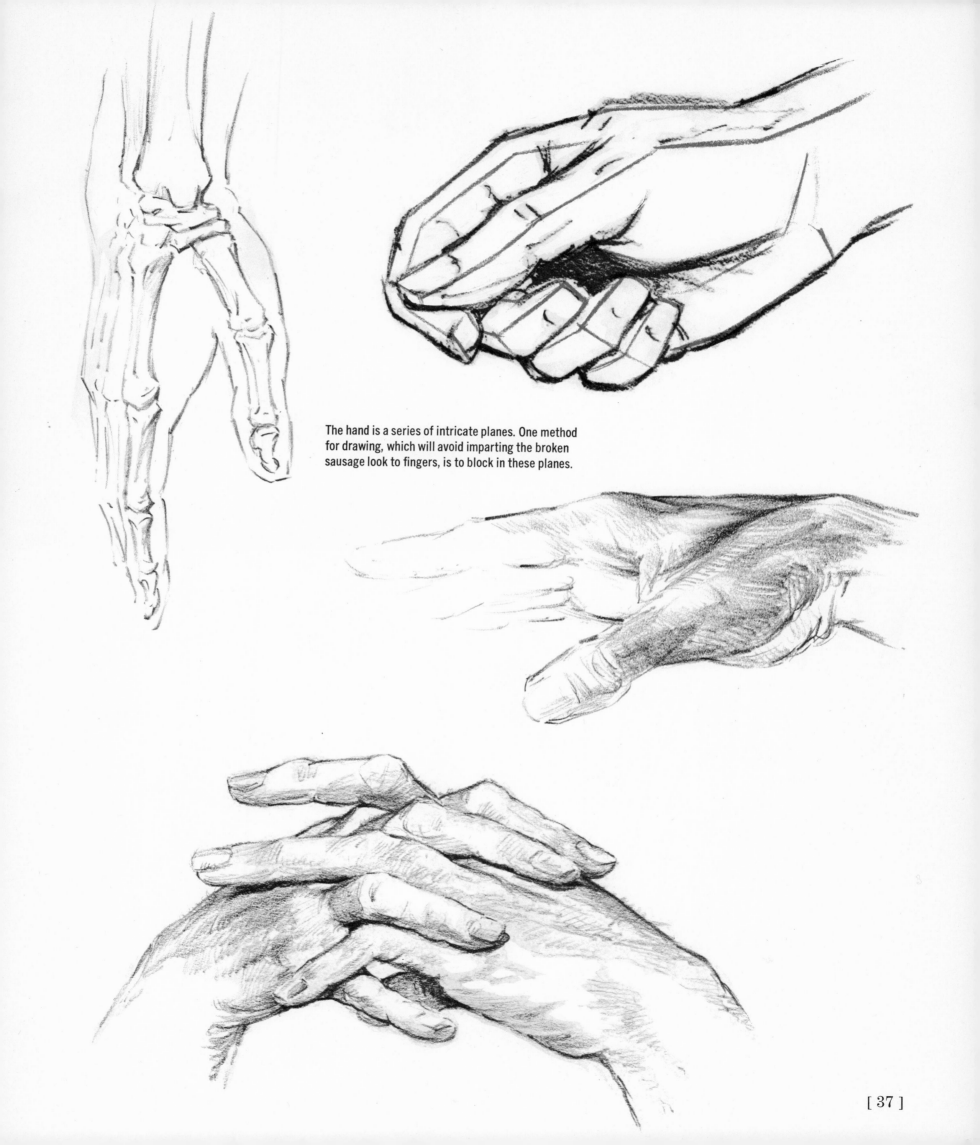

The hand is a series of intricate planes. One method for drawing, which will avoid imparting the broken sausage look to fingers, is to block in these planes.

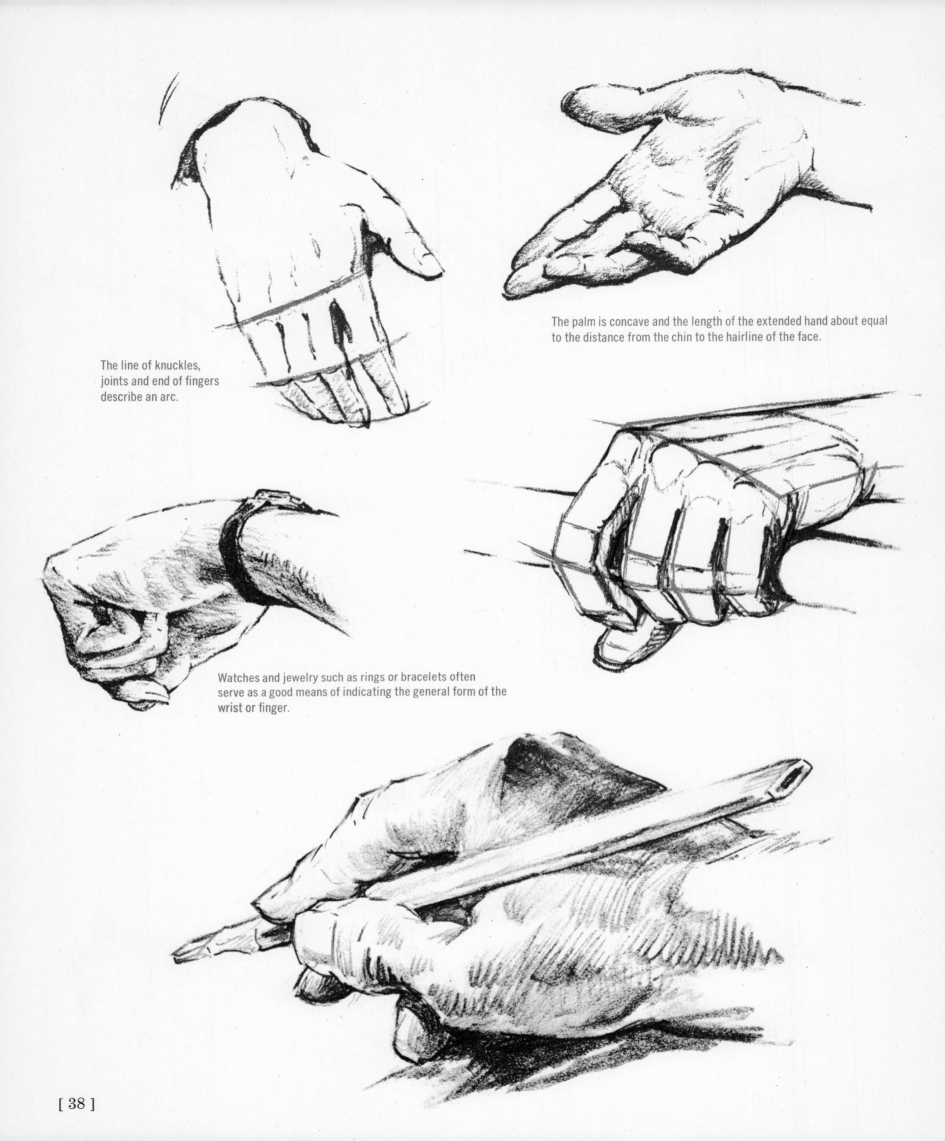

The line of knuckles, joints and end of fingers describe an arc.

The palm is concave and the length of the extended hand about equal to the distance from the chin to the hairline of the face.

Watches and jewelry such as rings or bracelets often serve as a good means of indicating the general form of the wrist or finger.

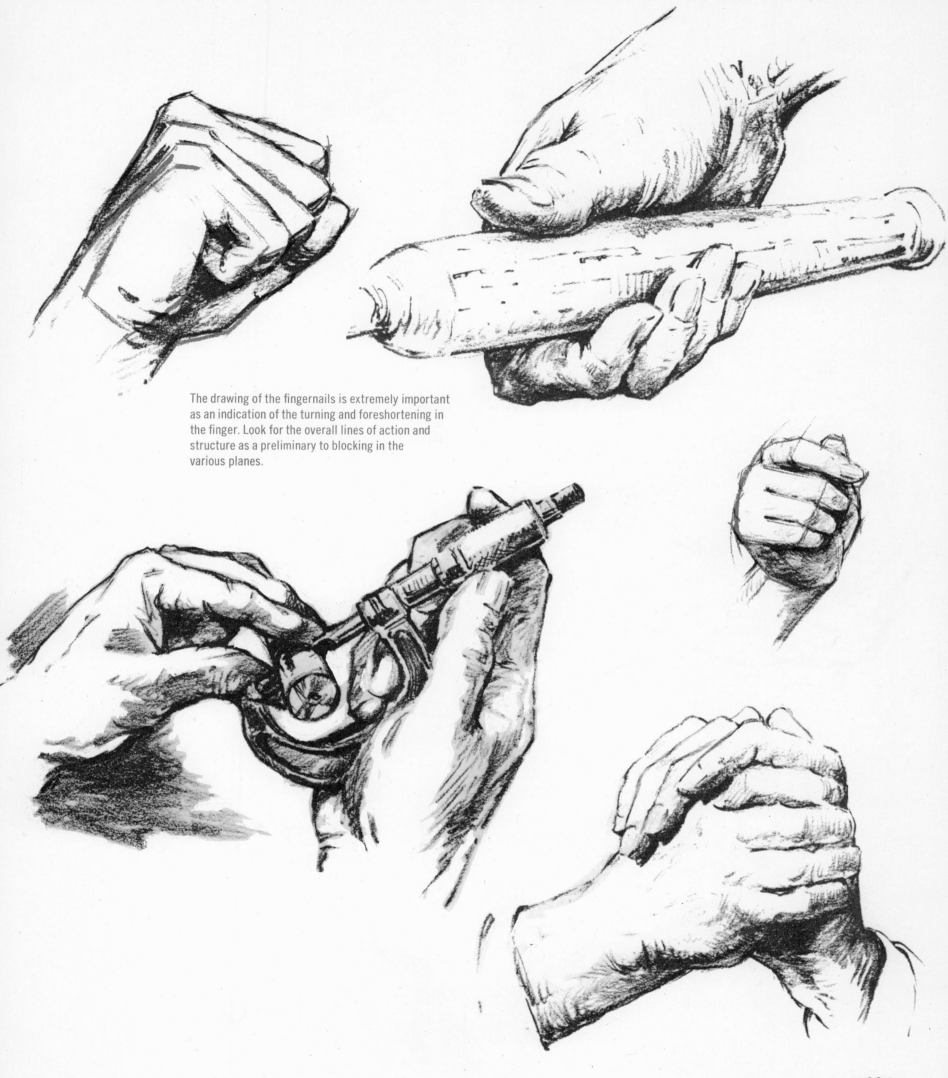

The drawing of the fingernails is extremely important as an indication of the turning and foreshortening in the finger. Look for the overall lines of action and structure as a preliminary to blocking in the various planes.

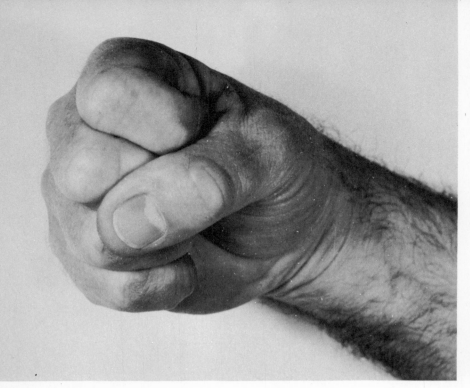

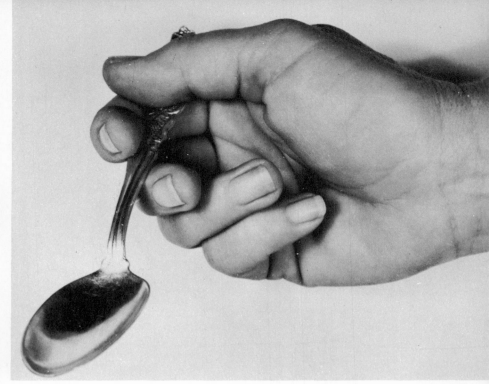

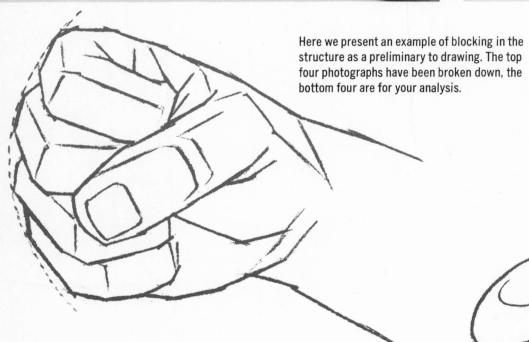

Here we present an example of blocking in the structure as a preliminary to drawing. The top four photographs have been broken down, the bottom four are for your analysis.

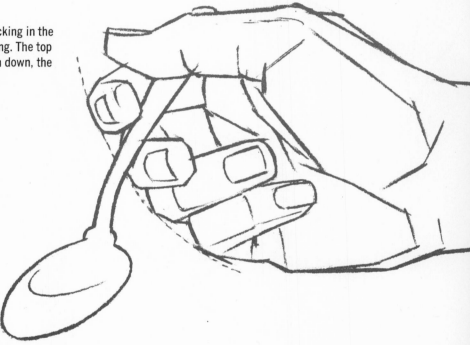

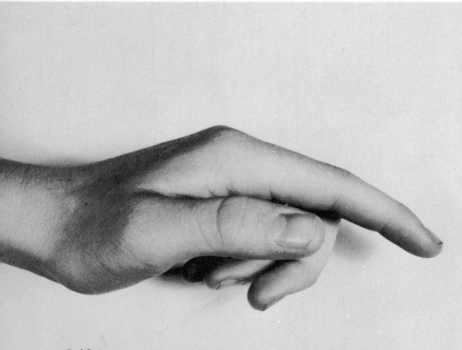

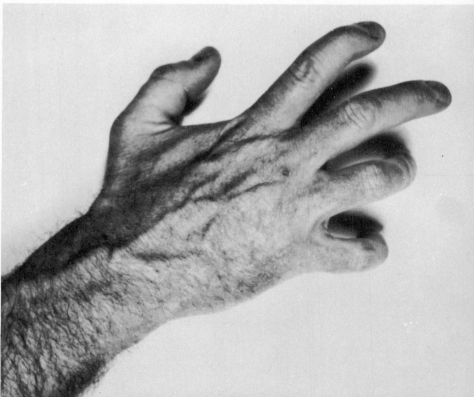

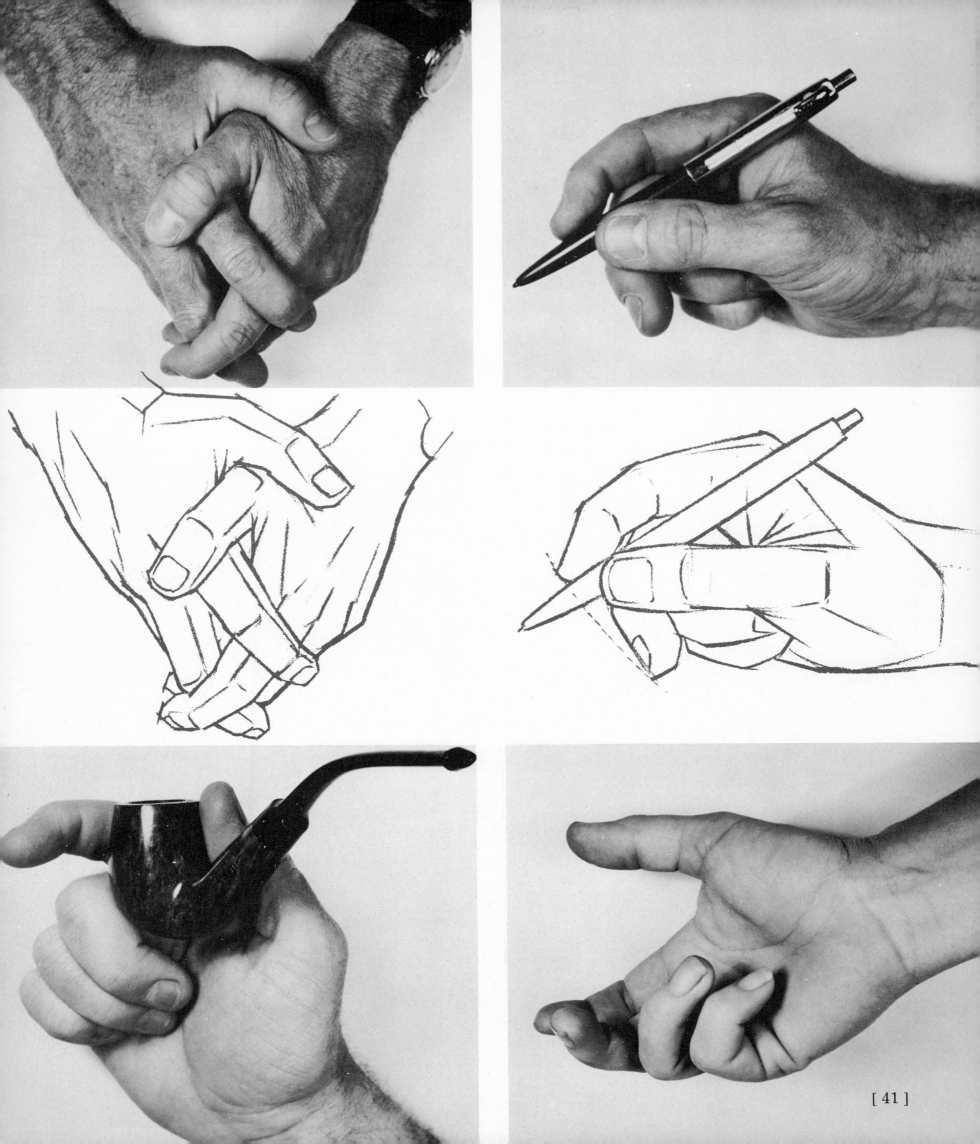

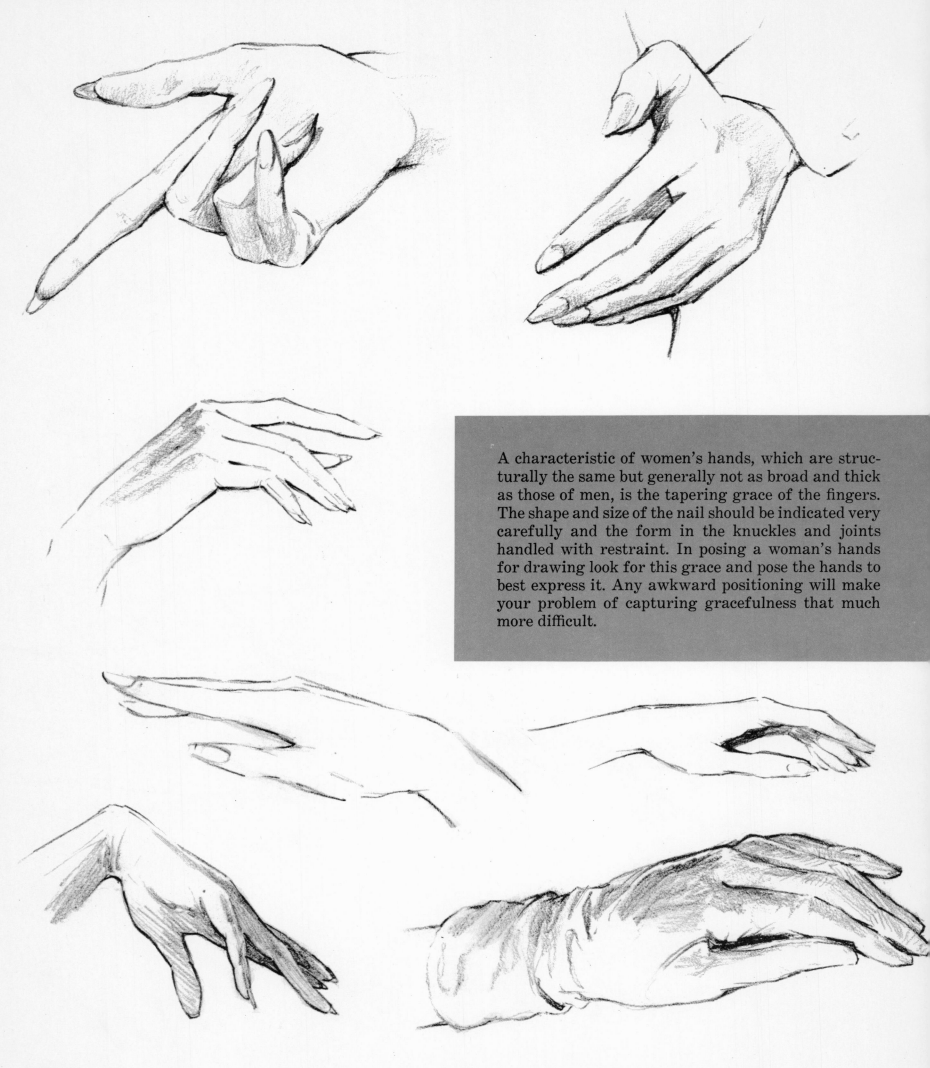

A characteristic of women's hands, which are structurally the same but generally not as broad and thick as those of men, is the tapering grace of the fingers. The shape and size of the nail should be indicated very carefully and the form in the knuckles and joints handled with restraint. In posing a woman's hands for drawing look for this grace and pose the hands to best express it. Any awkward positioning will make your problem of capturing gracefulness that much more difficult.

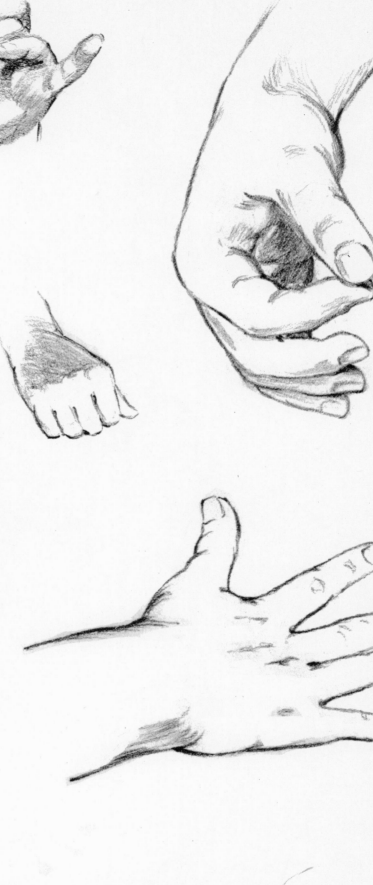

Babies and young children's hands have a roundness to the form. Fingers which have not yet developed are much shorter in relation to the palm so they take on a stubby appearance. In your observation look for specific characteristics such as the series of dimples which appear at the ridge of the knuckles when the hand is spread out. Structure and form in the knuckles and joints must be indicated without a great deal of emphasis or the hand will take on a much older look.

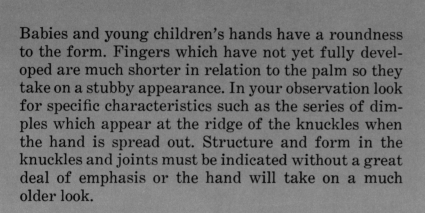

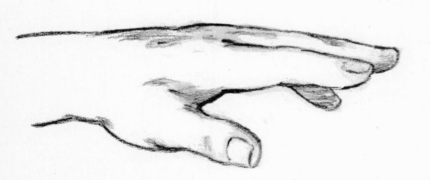

When working from photographs, it is very often necessary to indicate form with line where the camera does it with value. Always there is the matter of selection and emphasis. The camera sees and records everything, often with a degree of distortion. A subtle distortion, acceptable in the photograph, becomes grotesque when translated to a drawing and must be corrected.

In this charcoal drawing the dark area is handled very simply with very little change of value. The strong light on the face washes out detail in the light area. Squinting eyes are merely suggested rather than completely delineated.

This interesting study plays a strong light from both sides; all detail is kept to the center making a strong vertical.

This is a study demonstrating
the manner in which wrinkles follow
underlying muscle structure.

Use a judicious balance between
lights and darks to achieve emphasis.
It is important to consider the
source of light and the direction
of cast shadows.

When you have drawings to do for reproduction on greeting cards or assignments for clubs or local civic groups you will find Grumbacher Repro Boards wonderful to work on. When they are used properly it makes reproduction much simpler and less expensive. These are embossed papers, the texture of which breaks your drawing into a series of solid black dots, close to- gether or spread out depending on how hard you press your pencil to the paper. The best pencil to use for this technique is the "Cartoonist" crayon pencil. You can use brush and ink with these papers for fine lines or solid black areas with very sharp edges. Political and sports cartoonists utilize these boards for newspaper reproduction.

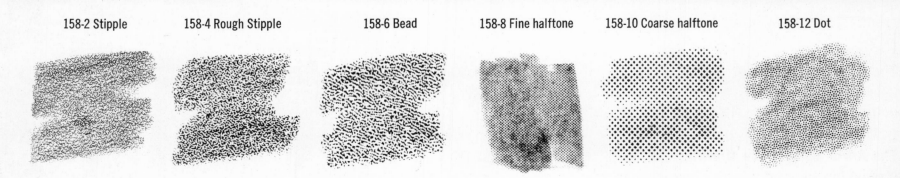

158-2 Stipple 158-4 Rough Stipple 158-6 Bead 158-8 Fine halftone 158-10 Coarse halftone 158-12 Dot